W9-CDA-751

THE GOLD OF FRIENDSHIP

THE GOLD OF FRIENDSHIP

A Bouquet of Special Thoughts

Selected by Patricia Dreier

The C.R. Gibson Company
Norwalk, Connecticut

GARLAND FOR FRIENDSHIP

Friendship is a country,
Of the young and young-in-heart,
Made of morning's greetings,
A warm and lovely part
Of phone calls and cups of tea,
Of days of hope and caring,
Friendship is sturdy refuge,
Forgiveness and sweet sharing
Memories and happy times,
Picnics, fun together,
Count among life's garlands
Friends who make heart's weather.

Gladys McKee

Oh, the comfort, the inexpressible comfort of feeling safe with a person; having neither to weigh thoughts nor measure words, but to pour them all out, just as they are, chaff and grain together, knowing that a faithful hand will take and sift them, keep what is worth keeping and then, with the breath of kindness, blow the rest away.

Dinah Maria Mulock Craik

I HAVE SEEN

I have seen the morning shining fair
    atop a green-clad hill
A robin perched so saucily
    upon my windowsill,
A valley where a little stream just seems
    to trickle through,
A sunset at the close of day, amidst a sky
    of blue.

I have seen a small forget-me-not,
    unnoticed by the rest,
A sparkling little dewdrop that a rosebud
    loves the best;
A dandelion growing where it naught shall come
    to harm,
A peaceful little pathway where no soul
    shall feel alarm.

I have often seen tomorrow as it smiles
 across the way,
The doubts and fears of living that are part
 of each today,
A promise soon forgotten and a word
 so lightly said,
A broken heart that's longing for a treasure
 long since dead.

I have seen a faith unfailing and a hope
 that lives through all
The loveliness of springtime and the
 melancholy fall;
All the beauties life can offer, all the heartaches
 life must send . . .
I have seen God's world of sunshine; I have shared
 it with a friend.

Garnett Ann Schultz

The glory of friendship is not the outstretched hand,
nor the kindly smile, nor the joy of companionship;
it is the spiritual inspiration that comes to one when
he discovers that someone believes in him and is
willing to trust him with his friendship.

Ralph Waldo Emerson

FRIENDSHIP

There are marvelous joys in friendship. This is easily understood as soon as one realizes that joy is contagious. If my presence gives a friend some real happiness, the sight of his happiness is enough to make me in turn feel happy; thus the joy that each of us gives is returned to him; at the same time, vast reserves of joy are released; both friends say to themselves: "I had happiness in me that I wasn't making use of."

The source of happiness is within us, I'll admit that; and there is nothing sadder to see than people dissatisfied with themselves and with everything else, and who have to tickle each other in order to be able to laugh. However, it must be added that a happy man quickly forgets that he is happy once he is alone; all his joy soon becomes numbed; he sinks into a kind of unawareness bordering on stupor. An inner feeling needs an external form of manifestation. If some tyrant or other imprisoned me in order to teach me respect for the mighty, I would make it a rule of good health to laugh every day all alone; I would exercise my joy just as I would exercise my legs.

Here is a bundle of dry branches. They seem as inert as earth; if you leave them there, they will become earth. However, locked within them is a hidden ardor which they captured from the sun. Bring the smallest flame near them and soon you will have a crackling fire. All you had to do was rattle the door and awaken the prisoner.

In the same way, there must be a kind of starting

signal to awaken joy. When a baby laughs for the first time, his laughter expresses nothing at all; he is not laughing because he is happy; instead, I should say that he is happy because he is laughing; he enjoys laughing, just as he enjoys eating, but first he has to try eating. This is not only true for laughter; one needs words in order to know what one is thinking. As long as one is alone, one cannot be oneself. Simple-minded moralists say that loving means forgetting yourself; that is too simplistic; the more you get away from yourself, the more you are yourself; and the more you feel alive. Don't let your wood rot in the cellar.

Alain

There is in friendship something of all relations, and something above them all. It is the golden thread that ties the hearts of all hearts of all the world.

John Evelyn

THE EVER OPEN DOOR

What shall I bestow upon a friend? Gay laughter to
sustain him when sorrow may bring pain? A bright song
of life, belief that winter ends in the glory of spring, a
prayer of hope for peace that will ever stay.

What shall I bestow upon a friend? Songs from my heart
which I've hidden away? Friendship that flowers, once
it enters the heart, spring's eternal loveliness, knowledge that love is a precious thing.

What shall I bestow upon a friend? Fleeting moments of
silent blessings? Trust in tomorrow, which is life's hardest
task, faith that each new dawn brings daylight's golden
pathways to the ever-open door, belief that God will be
with him though all others go their way.

Lea Palmer

A FRIEND

Crossing the uplands of time,
Skirting the borders of night,
Scaling the face of the peak of dreams,
We enter the region of light,
And hastening on with eager intent,
Arrive at the rainbow's end,
And here uncover the pot of gold
Buried deep in the heart of a friend.

Grace Goodhue Coolidge

WORDS FROM "THE PROPHET"
. . . ON FRIENDSHIP

And a youth said, Speak to us of Friendship.
And he answered, saying:
Your friend is your needs answered.
He is your field which you sow with love and reap
with thanksgiving.
And he is your board and your fireside.
For you come to him with your hunger, and you
seek him for peace.

When your friend speaks his mind you fear not the
"nay" in your own mind, nor do you withhold the "ay."
And when he is silent, your heart ceases not to listen
to his heart;
For without words, in friendship, all thoughts, all
desires, all expectations are born and shared, with joy
that is unacclaimed.
When you part from your friend, you grieve not;
For that which you love most in him may be clearer
in his absence, as the mountain to the climber is clearer
from the plain.

And let there be no purpose in friendship save the deepening of the spirit.

For love that seeks aught but the disclosure of its own mystery is not love but a net cast forth: and only the unprofitable is caught.

And let your best be for your friend.

If he must know the ebb of your tide, let him know its flood also.

For what is your friend that you should seek him with hours to kill?

Seek him always with hours to live.

For it is his to fill your need, but not your emptiness.

And in the sweetness of friendship let there be laughter, and sharing of pleasures.

For in the dew of little things the heart finds its morning and is refreshed.

Kahlil Gibran

THE THINGS I PRIZE

These are the things I prize
    And hold of dearest worth:
Light of the sapphire skies,
Peace of the silent hills,
Shelter of the forests, comfort of the grass,
Music of birds, murmur of little rills,
Shadows of clouds that swiftly pass,
    And, after showers,
    The smell of flowers
And of the good brown earth—
And best of all, along the way, friendship and mirth.

Henry van Dyke

SPECIAL PEOPLE

There are red-letter days in our lives when we meet
people who thrill us like a fine poem, people whose
handshake is brimful of unspoken sympathy and whose
sweet, rich natures impart to our eager, impatient spirits
a wonderful restfulness which is in its essence divine . . . .
Perhaps we never saw them before and they may never
cross our life's path again; but the influence of their calm,
mellow natures is a libation poured upon our discontent,
and we feel its healing touch as the ocean feels the
mountain stream freshening its brine . . . .

Helen Keller

THE BEST IS FREE AND NEAR

At the apple orchard we once owned there lived a child who seemed to be part of all the outdoor world around her. In summer she was brown as the hard-baked earth; her curly hair was a tangled auburn mass above her round, ten-year-old face. The skin of her square little hands and bare feet was tough as saddle leather. She knew where the cardinals and brown thrashers nested, where lady's-slippers grew and chipmunks hid; and treasures of tender cress or juicy berries or spicy herbs were her special knowledge.

One morning in spring she led me to a big old apple tree in one corner of the orchard. There, where the ground was rich and shaded, she knelt down carefully and folded back the tall grass with gentle hands, revealing clusters of ripe red strawberries.

After letting me pick a handful and enjoy their flavor for myself, she produced a small panful already picked and presented them to me, shyly and proudly. "They're plumb dripping with shu-gar," she cooed, and the way she elongated the word and savored it brought the taste of sweetness to my tongue again.

The following day we entertained at lunch a distinguished couple from other regions. For dessert I gave them some of my little friend's berries.

"Fraises des bois!" the husband exclaimed. "Very *recherché.* Delicious!"

So these world-traveled gourmets and a mountain child who had traveled only, as Thoreau had, extensively in her own back yard, shared a connoisseur's pleasure of one of nature's gifts. So often the best is free and near—if only we will part the grass and look.

Wilma Dykeman

HAPPINESS

Happiness is something more
Than what a man lays by in store,
More than prestige, more than power
Or fleeting pleasures of the hour.

Happiness is kindness living
In friendly hearts, in selfless giving,
A will to feel with one another
And treat a neighbor as a brother.

It is a faith, the nobler plan
That seeks the good in every man,
That leaves all censure unexpressed,
Forgives the flaw and sees the best!

Happiness is gold refined
Within the heart, a state of mind,
No need to travel, near or far,
You seek and find it—where you are!

A.G. Walton

TO A FRIEND

Because you are my friend
I long today
To bring you some imperishable gift
Of beauty:

Something glowing and warm
Like the coals of living fire,
Something as cool and sweet
As blue lilies at dawn,
Something as restful and clean
As smooth white sheets at night
When one is very tired,
Something with the taste of spring water
From high places,
Or like the tang of cool purple grapes
To the mouth.

But O my friend,
Since I cannot buy such gifts for you,
Come go with me
Out into the little everyday fields of living,
And let us gather in our baskets, like manna,
God's gift to us:

The down-pouring, exquisite beauty
Of life itself!

Grace Noll Crowell

TO BE A FRIEND

A good friend, it seems to me, is someone who knows what to do for you, without being asked, when you are in trouble. We all know the other sort of person, among whom I am afraid I must include myself, who says to someone in trouble, "Let me know if there is anything I can do." And we all know the answer to that one, too, usually from personal experience. It is, "Thank you, I will," whereupon we go off to wrestle with the demons by ourselves.

I am prompted to these reflections by a recent experience when Kitty was ill. She wasn't seriously ill. She wasn't sick enough to require a nurse, but she was supposed to be off her feet for a while.

"Let me know if there is anything I can do," Kitty's friends said to me, and our friends said to me.

"Thank you, I will," I said, and when they had gone it was all there staring at me, the empty house, and especially the kitchen; the shrine from which the goddess had fled.

Whatever had happened, I wondered, to the aunts and the cousins and the nieces and the vaguely related spinster ladies who used to come in and help under similar circumstances in the old days when we were children? Where had they all gone? Well, it was useless to speculate about that. I went to the pad clipped to the bulletin board behind the kitchen door, and began to make out a grocery list. The cupboard was bare. While Kitty was in the hospital I had eaten out, and everything in the refrigerator was either gone or spoiled.

It all seemed easy enough at first. (But I will anticipate what happened by saying that I learned something rather peculiar about the keeping of a household, which increases my respect for all women who do, by saying that no matter what I bought, or how much I bought, there was never anything in the refrigerator to eat.) I listed eggs and bacon and bread and orange juice and coffee. That took care of breakfast. Kitty suggested that in the evening we have TV dinners, and I was willing to go along with that as a last resort, but surely I could broil steak, and put potatoes in the oven, and heat a frozen vegetable.

And that went well enough for a day or so. The only trouble was that, as I have said, whenever I opened the refrigerator door it was still empty, and what did you do about lunch? I had worked at home in my study for years, and lunch had never been a crisis on any day that I could remember. Even when Kitty went to town to shop and left me to forage for myself, I could depend on opening that refrigerator door to find, instead of empty space, a variety of things from which I might choose to make up my own lunch. . . .By what magic had these objects always appeared, and where were they now? After I had carried dinner upstairs, and faithfully brought the dishes down again, and scraped them and put them in the dishwasher, I went back upstairs with the sinking feeling that next day I would have to start over again from scratch. It would be a ham-sandwich-for-lunch day again, if I remembered to call the grocer in time.

Then, on the evening of the fourth day, as I stood in the kitchen by the stove, staring at a block of frozen chow mein, trying to figure out what you were supposed to do about that, the telephone rang. It was

Mrs. Randolph, a new neighbor in back of us.

"It's Mimi," she said, "Mimi Randolph.". . .

"Have you already prepared your dinner?" Mrs. Randolph asked apparently knowing, by the underground, that I was the temporary chef.

"Well, not exactly," I said, staring at the frozen chow mein, and then putting it down to see if I could restore the circulation in that hand by rubbing it against my trousers.

"I've made a lamb stew," Mimi Randolph said, speaking quickly, and sort of shyly, as if she were afraid she might be out of order and wanted to hurry on before she would be rebuffed. "I've put in enough for two more, and if you will wait just fifteen minutes the biscuits will be done and Chris and I will run over with it."

"Oh, you shouldn't do that," I said. My tone was extremely unconvincing, and I felt a grin cracking my tired face.

"Why, it's nothing," Mimi Randolph said. "I just added to the pot." And then she hung up.

I went to the kitchen door and turned on the back light. It had begun to rain a bit, and I waited, and soon I saw the light go on at the kitchen door of the Randolphs, and two figures, one much smaller than the other, scudded, giggling, through the back way in the rain: Mimi and her small son, Chris. They were breathless and laughing and a little damp when they arrived at the door. They had a garden basket, and in it was a covered casserole, and a package of fresh, hot biscuits, wrapped in aluminum foil.

"Just put them both in the oven for a minute," Mimi said.

"You're awfully kind," I said. "Won't you come in?"

"Oh, thank you, we can't," Mimi said. "I have to feed Chris and Luisa, and Bob will be home any minute."

"I can't tell you how grateful we are," I said, taking the garden basket. "It certainly beats frozen chow mein."

"Tomorrow is baking day," Mimi said, turning at the door. "I'll bring you a loaf of bread."

"Oh, you mustn't do that," I said, not meaning it at all.

But they were gone, running in the rain. Chris's little knees were pumping up and down like pistons, and halfway across our lawn in back he threw his arms up, stiff, and uttered a kind of happy war cry, and Mimi laughed and chased him, and they disappeared through the hedge.

It was awfully good lamb stew. It was awfully good to taste something once again made by a practiced and loving hand. I carried the dishes down and tidied up and put things away the best I could, and next day, lo and behold, when I opened the refrigerator door, there was the remainder of the lamb stew in the casserole, waiting, for lunch.

"But you mustn't take the casserole back," Kitty said, when we finished it up for lunch. "When I'm on my feet again I'll make something to put in it, to take to them."

And I suppose it was at that moment that I began to see what it is to be a good friend. You must know how to do for others, without being asked, when they are in trouble. It is up to you to make that first step. You must carry the bowl, full, before you can expect to have it returned to you, full, again.

Bentz Plagemann

NEIGHBORS

Across the road, white napkin-spread,
Goes Mrs. Brown's banana bread;
And back, within a week at most—
Croquettes from Mrs. Johnson's roast.

Like clockwork, past the picket gate,
(And always on the same blue plate)
Corn fritters, corn sticks, corn pone vie
With apple fritters—jelly—pie.

For twenty years the plate has passed;
For twenty more the game will last—
Which one would stop it? For that matter,
Who knows who owns the Passing Platter?

Philene Hammer

BEGIN THE DAY

Begin the day with friendliness *and only friends you'll find*. . . Yes, greet the dawn with happiness, *keep happy thoughts in mind*. . . Salute the day with peaceful thoughts *and peace will fill your heart*. . . Begin the day with joyful soul *and joy will be your part*. . . Begin the day with friendliness, *keep friendly all day long*. . . Keep in your soul a friendly thought, *your heart a friendly song*. . . Have in your mind a word of cheer *for all who come your way*. . . And they will bless you too, in turn, *and wish you "Happy day!"*. . . Begin each day with friendly thoughts *and as the day goes on*. . . Keep friendly, loving, good and kind *just as you were at dawn*. . . The day will be a friendly one *and then at night you'll find*. . . That you were happy all day long *through friendly thoughts in mind*.

Author Unknown

FRIEND

A warm handclasp,
A fond embrace,
A friendly smile
When face to face—
A cheerful greeting
Which seems to say
That you're concerned
This makes my day.

I sense a gladness
When we meet
Upon the stair
Or on the street.
Your sparkling eye—
This simple act
Makes glad my heart,
Now, that's a fact.

Louis Everett Downing

GOD GIVE ME JOY

God give me joy in the common things:
In the dawn that lures, the eve that sings.

In the new grass sparkling after rain,
In the late wind's wild and weird refrain;

In the springtime's spacious field of gold,
In the precious light by winter doled.

God give me joy in the love of friends,
In their dear home talk as summer ends;

In the songs of children, unrestrained;
In the sober wisdom age has gained.

God give me joy in the tasks that press,
In the memories that burn and bless;

In the thought that life has love to spend,
In the faith that God's at journey's end.

God give me hope for each day that springs,
God give me joy in the common things!

Thomas Curtis Clark

WHAT MORNING MEANS

Think of living in a world where there are no mornings! Then there would be no opalescent glow along the horizon as the first light begins to appear, no stirring of birds in country woods, no accelerating beat as the tempo of city life increases, no smell of dew on grass in summer or an unblemished snowfall that came during a winter night.

The Psalmist has said, "Weeping may endure for a night but joy cometh in the morning."

We may weep for all our yesterdays and their shortcomings during the night, but doesn't the morning bring hope for today and its potential?

The world shows a fresh face to those who travel early in the morning. Sometimes there is fog. The dense swirling curtain shrouds you in a world alone. Other infrequent vehicles pass like ghosts. Nothing is visible beyond the boundaries of the highway. Then the first rays of the sun begin to burn away the fog.

In some parts of the country you begin to pass farmers on their way to barn and field and you see the livestock waiting to greet them—cows, horses, chickens, pigs, guineas—all hungry. Once in a while smoke even curls from a kitchen chimney.

Or, in the West, in the great woods there are all sorts of animals to be encountered early in the morning—heavy-antlered elk, bear, deer, porcupine, even a moose. And in the desert there is the first shaft of sunrise tipping a sudden butte or mesa, the occasional movement of an animal or man dwarfed by the enormity of space.

And in the towns the first tradespeople open their doors, sweep sidewalks, exchange greetings with friends, gulp coffee at the all-night café. But wherever you observe early morning there hovers this sense of a fresh beginning.

It has been said, "Only that day dawns to which we are awake." Daylight can come over the hill or across the plain or above the skyline three hundred and sixty-five times, but unless we are aware of the meaning of the morning we shall have been dead for a year.

And somewhere on this planet morning is always just arriving. Always we are traveling to meet ourselves.

Wilma Dykeman

HAPPINESS

Man strives for glory, honor, fame,
That all the world may know his name.
Amasses wealth by brain and hand;
Becomes a power in the land,
But when he nears the end of life
And looks back over the years of strife,
He finds that happiness depends
On none of these but love of friends.

Author Unknown

THE BLESSING OF FRIENDSHIP

A blessed thing it is for any man or woman to have a friend; one human soul whom we can trust utterly; who knows the best and the worst of us, and who loves us in spite of all our faults; who will speak the honest truth to us, while the world flatters us to our face, and laughs at us behind our back; who will give us counsel and reproof in the day of prosperity and self-conceit; but who, again, will comfort and encourage us in the day of difficulty and sorrow, when the world leaves us alone to fight our own battle as we can.

Charles Kingsley

FRIENDS ARE NOT A ONE-WAY STREET

A few weeks ago in New York an old and valued friend remarked, "I don't bother with anyone who bores me. I have cut down all my contacts to a minimum, I see only those people whom I really enjoy."

With the instantaneous reaction of the very busy I thought for a moment, how wonderful. To have matters so arranged that one would be spared the countless contacts that often seem frantically and futilely time-consuming.

And yet, on reflection, I'm not so sure.

Aren't friendships, on whatever level, a part of human fortune? Friendships can be infinitely varied. And by their very differentness the whole pattern of one's days can be enlivened, and in so many ways rewarding.

Sift through your friendships; sort them.

There is the rich inner circle of those people who are dearest to the heart. Usually these are the persons to whom we can most honestly express our deepest selves. And even though we may not see them for days, weeks on end—even years—the bond remains strong and special and true.

Yet would we not be the poorer without the infinite variety of others?

Friends can be friends for so many different reasons. There is the wonderfully helpful neighbor who is always willing to give you a hand with the children, or whip up a skirt for you.

There is the witty one who can always make you laugh.

There is the one who sends over bones for the dog, and is generous with praise for your growing crew.

There is the quiet soul who occasionally comes up with a startling gem of philosophy.

It takes patience sometimes to appreciate the true values in the people with whom circumstances have surrounded us. It takes awareness to recognize these values when they appear.

Yet almost everyone has something uniquely his own to contribute to our lives—and equally important, a place in his own life that perhaps we alone can satisfy.

The heart has many doors. Don't be too quick to bolt them.

Marjorie Holmes

OLD FRIENDSHIP

Beautiful and rich is an old friendship,
    Grateful to the touch as ancient ivory,
Smooth as aged wine, or sheen of tapestry
    Where light has lingered,
        intimate and long.
Full of tears and warm is an old friendship
    That asks no longer deeds of gallantry,
Or any deed at all—
        save that the friend shall be
Alive and breathing somewhere,
        like a song.

Eunice Tietjens

*Friends are for the best of times. . . especially when they
are lifelong friends and you really enjoy each other and
can't wait to catch up. Dorothy Van Doren, wife of the late
poet-professor, Mark Van Doren, speaks from the heart as
she speaks of friends. For her, as for so many of us,
familiar faces breed loving times, which are the best of
times.*

    A while ago my husband and I made a trip to San
Francisco. We spent the night with a couple we have
known for more than thirty years, the man having
been a student of my husband's. We used to see them
often, regularly in New York and every summer when
they were our nearest neighbors in Connecticut; but
in the last ten, maybe fifteen years, since they moved
west, I don't believe I have seen either of them half a
dozen times.

The visit was a great success. We found we had lots to talk about, not only to catch up with our respective lives since we had seen each other, but in general, about all sorts of subjects, on which as we used to do we more or less agreed. We were still talking busily when it was time to go to bed and we kept coming out of our bedrooms for another remark; finally we were all four out in the hall in various stages of undress, still talking sixteen to the dozen.

In the morning I asked the wife how they liked living in San Francisco. It was a beautiful city, she said, and that was plain to see; they had met some agreeable people; they enjoyed the climate, the view of the Bay, the cosmopolitan character of the place. "It's very nice to live in really," she said. "Only of course there are no old friends. At our age you don't make friends the way you used to; there isn't time."

I have often thought of what she said. Old friends. Among our own friends are a number I knew in college or met soon after; a greater number we both met during our first New York jobs, all this being some four decades ago. We still see them, not as often as we did surely, but in any sort of exceptional situation, good or bad; if my husband receives an honor for instance or if we go through a period of strain and difficulty, we hear from them. They don't necessarily say much when they write or telephone.

Quite often they simply send us their love.

We have lived long enough in our Connecticut town to have old friends, too. People we met the magic winter of our first sabbatical leave; people we got to know soon after. We sometimes get together with the sabbatical-winter friends and laugh about old times; the night the men got to playing chess and after a while they went outdoors and one of them said. "What's that light over there in the sky?" "That," replied another, "is the sun coming up." It was late winter, so the time was between six and seven in the morning. It was the time when our children were babies or small children; we look at our grandchildren now and remember those days with wry fondness. We remember square dances and evening picnics at the lake and going swimming by moonlight and getting stuck in the mud in the spring and things like that. We remember them together, because we have known each other for a long time. It would be hard, probably, for our younger friends whom we have not known so long to think of us doing the gay or foolish things they themselves do. We did them; and our old friends know it.

We went to a holiday party recently. It was a pleasant party and our hosts were old friends, too. But they have moved away and their guests were almost all strange to us. They were friendly people and easy to talk to, of course; but on the way home we said somehow the parties at home were more fun. People we see all the time, nothing new or surprising about them; we know when we can talk politics with them because they think as we do and when we can't unless we want to get into an exhausting and meaningless argument. We are likely to exchange gifts at Christmas and birthdays, gifts we have made ourselves maybe, some of us being much more clever than others at making things. It doesn't matter; it is the feeling of being old friends that matters.

Long ago some of our friends had a conversation about us which they later reported. We, they said, were among all their acquaintances the ones who most definitely had roots, who had stayed put, who could be counted on to be living in the same place next year or the year after. I was not sure then nor am I now that this is a good thing, but I expect it is true.

For us, we live the life we like. We like familiar objects, we like the same house. I go so far as to like the same way of placing furniture, but my children correct me on this. Most particularly we like the same friends; the ones we have known for quite a while. We like to get together with them at their houses or at our house, eat dinner, sit by the fire, and talk. We don't play bridge with them or canasta, we don't usually listen to music; we don't recite poetry or do charades (I hate charades). We just talk and after a while they go home or we do. I say it was a nice evening, wasn't it. A nice evening; rather a mild remark. But it was nice, it was pleasant, it was friend-ly. It was, indeed, full of love, unexpressed in ordi-nary times but in extraordinary times often clearly stated. In extraordinary times, in times of trouble, it is heart-moving to find how many old friends say they love you.

A FRIEND IS . . .

A friend is someone who helps you clean up the dishes and you don't even have to protest once.

. . . that one word "hello" over the phone that can make you feel better than 10 minutes of conversation with anyone else.

. . . deep talks that go on until 3 a.m. On a work night!

A friend is more than a shoulder to cry on. A friend is the kind of understanding that makes crying unnecessary.

. . . someone to call in a hurry when something really watchable is on TV.

. . . sharing a pizza.

A friend is someone you can do nothing with . . . and enjoy it.

. . . one good reason for believing in ESP.

. . . someone who won't say, "You look terrible!" when you look terrible.

A friend is the one who is already there doing it when everyone else is saying, "Is there anything I can do?"

. . . someone who will quietly destroy the snapshot that makes you look like the bride of Frankenstein.

. . . not too much sugar and just enough spice.

A friend is the kind of person who never wants to dress alike.

. . . someone who dislikes the same people you do.

. . . a little bit different every day but always the same.

A friend is someone who *really is* glad when you succeed.

. . . a believer in the spur of the moment.

. . . someone with whom you can either a borrower or a lender be.

A friend is a person who knows your sensitive spots but will never poke you there.

. . . a whole lot of wonderful people rolled into one.

. . . someone you can trade secrets with and never worry.

. . . laughter and going places and doing new things and having the best time ever.

A friend is the closest thing to me there is . . . in more ways than one.

Gayle Lawrence

THAT GOOD AND TIMELY DEED

Friendships do not come by chance. Upon the looms of circumstance Fate weaves an intricate design—and threads of other lives entwine to make a pattern with our own.

We were not made to walk alone. Our pathways lead to where we meet a friend in need. It seems that it was meant to be. And how important is that little touch of kindness at a time when it is needed most.

These are the kindnesses that you don't forget:

The gesture of true sympathy that's made in all sincerity and comes when you are weary or upset.

The understanding word that reaches down into your heart—at the very moment of your need.

A well-timed act of friendliness that saves you from despair—even though it may be small.

A good turn done for you that shows that someone has concern for you.

How much it really means—that good and timely deed!

The love that we appreciate is that which does not come too late to help us when we need it most of all!

Author Unknown

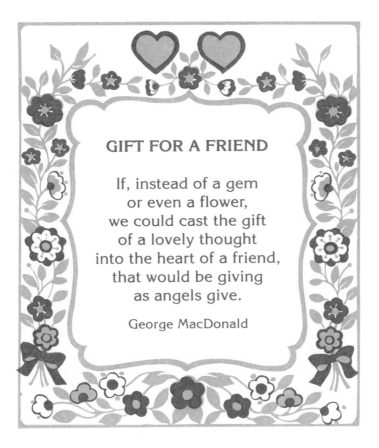

GIFT FOR A FRIEND

If, instead of a gem
or even a flower,
we could cast the gift
of a lovely thought
into the heart of a friend,
that would be giving
as angels give.

George MacDonald

WHAT IS A FRIEND?

A friend is someone tried and true,
That you can tell your troubles to,
A gentle smile, a happy face
That makes the world a better place.
A friend is someone that is yours
As long as time and life endures,
Sharing cherished moments when
You know you never need pretend.

A friend is someone "fair and square"
Who comforts just by being there,
A fellow-traveler who brings
New meaning to the "little things."
Who always has the time to say
A word to brighten up your day,
Who helps you to accomplish more
Than you have ever done before.

A friend brings out the best you are,
Within the darkest night . . . a star,
Throughout the greyest days a beam
Of sunlight stitched along each seam.
Who senses what you never say,
And somehow likes you just the way
You are, in spite of all you lack,
And each of us on looking back,

Recalls a voice, a special face
No other person can replace,
Who brushes back the doubt and care,
. . . Just because he's always there!
A prize that each of us must earn,
Who helps us grow and helps us learn,
Asking nothing save a part
Of tenderness within our heart.

Because they are of such a kind,
A friend like this is hard to find.
I think by now we all have seen
That they are "few and far between."
Heaven's Emissary, he
Who leads us toward Eternity . . .
Becoming a reflection of
God's deep and everlasting love.

Grace E. Easley

EVERYONE NEEDS FRIENDS

Without friends no one would choose to live,
though he had all other goods; even rich men and
those in possession of office and of dominating power
are thought to need friends most of all; for what is the
use of such prosperity without the opportunity of
beneficence, which is exercised chiefly and in its most
laudable form towards friends? Or how can prosperity
be guarded and preserved without friends? The
greater it is, the more exposed is it to risk. And in
poverty and in other misfortunes men think friends
are the only refuge. It helps the young, too, to keep
from error; it aids older people by ministering to their
needs and supplementing the activities that are failing
from weakness; those in the prime of life it stimulates
to noble actions. . . for with friends men are more
able both to think and to act.

Aristotle

WHAT IS LIFE WITHOUT A FRIEND?

Say not that friendship's but a name,
Sincere we none can find;
An empty bubble in the air,
A phantom of the mind.
What is life without a friend?
A dreary race to run,
A desert where no water is,
A world without a sun.

Henry Alford

There are three friendships which are advantageous,
and three which are injurious. Friendship with the
upright, with the sincere, and with the man of much
observation, these are advantageous. Friendship with
the man of specious airs, with the insinuatingly soft,
and with the glib-tongued, these are injurious.

Confucius

A TIME TO BE SILENT

There may be moments in friendship, as in love, when silence is beyond words. The faults of our friend may be clear to us, but it is well to seem to shut our eyes to them. Friendship is usually treated by the majority of mankind as a tough and everlasting thing which will survive all manner of bad treatment. But this is an exceedingly great and foolish error; it may die in an hour of a single unwise word; its conditions of existence are that it should be dealt with delicately and tenderly, being as it is a sensible plant and not a roadside thistle. We must not expect our friend to be above humanity.

Ouida

THE HOURS THAT TRULY COUNT

Life may scatter us and keep us apart; it may prevent us from thinking very often of one another; but we know that our comrades are somewhere "out there"—where, one can hardly say—silent, forgotten, but deeply faithful. And when our paths cross theirs, they greet us with such manifest joy, shake us so gaily by the shoulders! Indeed we are accustomed to waiting...

We forget that there is no hope of joy except in human relations. If I summon up those memories that have left with me an enduring savor, if I draw up the balance sheet of the hours in my life that have truly counted, surely I find only those that no wealth could have procured me. True riches cannot be bought.

Antoine de Saint-Exupéry

THE WEALTH OF FRIENDSHIP

There is no treasure which may be compared unto a
    faithful friend;
Gold soon decayeth, and worldly wealth consumeth,
    and wasteth in the wind;
But love once planted in a perfect and pure mind
    endureth weal and woe;
The frowns of fortune, come they never so unkind,
    cannot it overthrow.

Author Unknown

Because of a friend, life is a little stronger, fuller,
more gracious thing for the friend's existence,
whether he be near or far. If the friend is close at
hand, that is best; but if he is far away he still is there
to think of, to wonder about, to hear from, to write to,
to share life and experience with, to serve, to honor,
to admire, to love.

Arthur Christopher Benson

Four things are specially the property of friendship:
love and affection, security and joy. And four things
must be tried in friendship: faith, intention, discretion
and patience. Indeed, as the sage says, all men would
lead a happy life if only two tiny words were taken
from them, mine and thine.

Aelred of Rievaulx

ARITHMETIC

Count your garden by the flowers,
Never by the leaves that fall;
Count your days by golden hours,
Don't remember clouds at all.
Count your nights by stars, not shadows,
Count your years with smiles, not tears,
Count your blessings, not your troubles,
Count your age by friends, not years.

Author Unknown

FRIENDS ARE LIKE FLOWERS

Friends are like flowers. I have found them so:
The hardy staunch perennials that grow
Year after year are like some friends I know.

One need not cultivate them with great care,
They only need the sun and wind and air
Of trust and love, and they are always there . . .

Some must be nursed with frequent trowel and spade,
And sheltered from the sun, or too much shade,
For fear their frail and clinging bloom may fade.

Friends are like flowers. I would be a friend
Whose blossomings no hand need ever tend:
A perennial on whom hearts can depend.

Grace Noll Crowell

FRIENDSHIP

Friendship needs no studied phrases,
Polished face, or winning wiles;
Friendship deals no lavish praises,
Friendship dons no surface smiles.
Friendship follows Nature's diction,
Shuns the blandishments of Art,
Boldly severs truth from fiction,
Speaks the language of the heart.
Friendship—pure, unselfish friendship,
All through life's alloted span,
Nurtures, strengthens, widens, lengthens,
Man's relationship with man.

Author Unknown

A FRIEND IS . . .

On the level of the human spirit an equal, a companion, an understanding heart is one who can share a man's point of view. What this means we all know. Friends, companions, lovers, are those who treat us in terms of our unlimited worth to ourselves. They are closest to us who best understand what life means to us, who feel for us as we feel for ourselves, who are bound to us in triumph and disaster, who break the spell of our loneliness.

Henry Alonzo Myers

SURRENDER TO TIME

It may seem, looking back, that becoming a friend . . . takes place in an instant. If we examine the experience, however, we discover that a long preparation through time precedes those moments in which friends finally recognize and respond to each other. If we do not surrender to time, we may never recognize our true selves nor the true selves of others; we may not be able to enter those instants in which we see someone else in a way that no one else has ever seen them before. . . . Friends move toward each other through time. When they meet they are able to respond to all that they have come to recognize as valuable. Time is the tide that brings us together when we are ready for the challenge of friendship.

Eugene Kennedy

ALL LOSSES RESTORED

When to the sessions of sweet silent thought
I summon up remembrance of things past,
I sigh the lack of many a thing I sought,
And with old woes new wail my dear time's waste:
Then can I drown an eye, unused to flow,
For precious friends hid in death's dateless night,
And weep afresh love's long since cancell'd woe,
And moan the expense of many a vanish'd sight:
Then can I grieve at grievances foregone,
And heavily from woe to woe tell o'er
The sad account of fore-bemoaned moan,
Which I new pay as if not paid before.
But if the while I think on thee, dear friend,
All losses are restored and sorrows end.

William Shakespeare

In the following selection, Gladys Taber, the celebrated author of the Stillmeadow *books, discusses the loss of her friend Jill and the impact of friendship on her life.*

At the time I first faced the fact that I was to be alone, it did not seem to me I could develop any skill in managing anything. It was, in fact, quite hopeless. My life seemed as purposeless as a drifting sailboat. But I had a strong sense that I was now meeting the most difficult learning-time of my life, and it might be I could learn a little. I needed a personal star to steer by.

I found it in the assurance that I had a relationship with life because Jill was still an integral part of it. This cannot be explained; it is felt. My guide was to be the same steadfast love of the past years. And so I was not alone, although I might be solitary.

ALL LOSSES RESTORED

When to the sessions of sweet silent thought
I summon up remembrance of things past,
I sigh the lack of many a thing I sought,
And with old woes new wail my dear time's waste:
Then can I drown an eye, unused to flow,
For precious friends hid in death's dateless night,
And weep afresh love's long since cancell'd woe,
And moan the expense of many a vanish'd sight:
Then can I grieve at grievances foregone,
And heavily from woe to woe tell o'er
The sad account of fore-bemoaned moan,
Which I new pay as if not paid before.
But if the while I think on thee, dear friend,
All losses are restored and sorrows end.

William Shakespeare

In the following selection, Gladys Taber, the celebrated author of the Stillmeadow *books, discusses the loss of her friend Jill and the impact of friendship on her life.*

At the time I first faced the fact that I was to be alone, it did not seem to me I could develop any skill in managing anything. It was, in fact, quite hopeless. My life seemed as purposeless as a drifting sailboat. But I had a strong sense that I was now meeting the most difficult learning-time of my life, and it might be I could learn a little. I needed a personal star to steer by.

I found it in the assurance that I had a relationship with life because Jill was still an integral part of it. This cannot be explained; it is felt. My guide was to be the same steadfast love of the past years. And so I was not alone, although I might be solitary.

Working back into life, I found the greatest guide was friendship. There are two reasons for this: The more I shared the lives of friends, the less I concentrated on my own. The world opened out, wide and interesting. Secondly, I found it eased my heart to spend love (of which I seemed to have a great store). I had time, now, to make new friends, too, which had not been possible during Jill's illness. And sharing the happiness of others, as well as trying to help with sorrows, gave me a new sense of being a part of life itself.

Friendship is related to love, and if love is the bread of life, friendship is in the same package. And friendship is a very good guide. In fact, it seems to me the world situation, as I write, is partially due to a lack of willingness to make friends, to care about other people, other lands. This characterizes the rulers of many countries. If the nations could work at making friends, there would be no threat of war, ever again.

I could not rewrite history, of course, but I could let friendship be a guidepost for my life.

Friendship consists in forgetting what one gives, and remembering what one receives.

Alexandre Dumas

The love of friendship should be gratuitous. You ought not to have or to love a friend for what he will give you. If you love him for the reason that he will supply you with money or some other temporal favor, you love the gift rather than him. A friend should be loved freely for himself, and not for anything else.

St. Augustine

THE RAREST FAITH

Friendship takes place between those who have an affinity for one another, and is a perfectly natural and inevitable result. No professions or advances will avail. Even speech, at first, necessarily has nothing to do with it; but it follows after silence, as the buds in the graft do not put forth into leaves till long after the graft has taken. It is a drama in which the parties have no part to act . . . .

Friendship is never established as an understood relation. Do you demand that I be less your friend that you may know it? Yet what right have I to think that another cherishes so rare a sentiment for me? It is a miracle which requires constant proofs. It is an exercise of the finest imagination and the rarest faith. It says by a silent but eloquent behavior: "I will be so related to thee as thou canst not imagine; even so thou mayest believe. I will spend truth, all my wealth on thee," and the friend responds silently through his nature, and life, and treats his friend with the same divine courtesy. . . .

The language of Friendship is not words but meaning. It is an intelligence above language. One imagines endless conversations with his friend, in which the tongue shall be loosed, and thoughts be spoken, without hesitancy, or end; but the experience is commonly far otherwise. . . .

Suppose you go to bid farewell to your friend who is setting out on a journey; what other outward sign do you know than to shake his hand. . .? There are some things which a man never speaks of, which are much finer kept silent about. To the highest communications we only lend a silent ear. . . . In human intercourse the tragedy begins, not when there is misunderstanding about words, but when silence is not understood.

Henry David Thoreau

A FRIEND OR TWO

There's all of pleasure and all of peace
    In a friend or two;
And all your troubles may find release
    Within a friend or two;
It's in the grip of the sleeping hand
On native soil or in alien land,
But the world is made—do you understand—
    Of a friend or two.

A song to sing, and a crust to share
    With a friend or two;
A smile to give and a grief to bear
    With a friend or two;
A road to walk and goal to win,
An inglenook to find comfort in,
The gladdest hours that we know begin
    With a friend or two.

A little laughter; perhaps some tears
    With a friend or two;
The days, the weeks, and the months and years
    With a friend or two;
A vale to cross and a hill to climb,
A mock at age and a jeer at time—
The prose of life takes the lilt of rhyme
    With a friend or two.

The brother-soul and the brother-heart
    Of a friend or two
Make us drift on from the crowd apart,
    With a friend or two;
For come days happy or come days sad
We count no hours but the ones made glad
By the hale good times we have ever had
    With a friend or two.
Then brim the goblet and quaff the toast
    To a friend or two,
For glad the man who can always boast
    Of a friend or two;
But fairest sight is a friendly face,
The blithest tread is a friendly pace,
And heaven will be a better place
    For a friend or two.

                    Wilbur D. Nesbit

TO A FRIEND

I ask but one thing of you, only one,
    That always you will be my dream of you;
    That never shall I wake to find untrue
All this I have believed and rested on,
Forever vanished, like a vision gone
    Out into the night. Alas how few
    There are who strike in us a chord we knew
Existed, but so seldom heard its tone
    We tremble at the half-forgotten sound.
The world is full of rude awakenings
    And heaven-born castles shattered to the ground,
Yet still our human longing vainly clings
    To a belief in beauty through all wrongs.
    O stay your hand, and leave my heart its songs!

Amy Lowell

WITH MY LOVE AS OF OLD

The roads we chose diverged so little at the setting-
    out and seemed so nearly side by side!
A little while we spoke across the way, then waved
    our hands, and then . . .
The hills between, life's other voices and the nights,
The silences . . .

Old friend, no new friend takes your place.
    With me as well
The hours and days flow by and lengthen
    into years,
But I do not forget. And not a thought
    that you have had of me—
Whether you wrote or spoke it, or, more like,
Just thought of me and let it go at that—
But it came winging through the silences!

Wherever you are, across the distance I give
    you my hand,
With my love as of old.

                    John Palmer Gavit

FRIENDSHIP IS . . .

It is a sweet thing, friendship, a dear balm,
A happy and auspicious bird of calm,
Which rides o'er life's ever tumultuous Ocean;
A God that broods o'er chaos in commotion;
A flower which fresh as Lapland roses are,
Lifts its bold head into the world's frore air,
And blooms most radiantly when others die,
Health, hope, and youth, and brief prosperity;
And with the light and odour of its bloom,
Shining within the dungeon and the tomb;
Whose coming is as light and music are
'Mid dissonance and gloom—a star
Which moves not 'mid the moving heavens alone—
A smile among dark frowns—a gentle tone
Among rude voices, a beloved light,
A solitude, a refuge, a delight.

Percy Bysshe Shelley

FRIENDS COME, FRIENDS GO

Friends come, friends go; the loves
    men know are ever fleeting;
In song and smile a little while
    we read their kindly greeting;
With warmth and cheer they linger near,
    the friends we fondly treasure;
Then on a day they drift away,
    a loss no words can measure.
This much we know: friends come, friends go,
    as April's gladness passes,
As sun and shade, in swift parade,
    paint changes on meadow grasses.
And though we grieve to see them leave,
    in thought we still enfold them;
In Memory's Net we keep them yet,
    and thus can ever hold them.
They come, they go—these Loves we know.
    Life's Tides are ever moving;
But year on year, they still seem near—
    so great the power of loving.

Author Unknown

BEING A "BARGAIN" FRIEND

Lord, help me to be a "bargain" friend. By that I mean, let those who come to me for friendship get more than they expected.

For what they give me in friendship, Lord, let me remember to try to give them still more.

Let them always go away from me surprised at the fullness of their hearts.

Let them always be pleased at the measure they have received from me. And remind me never to put my thumb on the scale when I am weighing out my love to them.

Let me always put an extra something, an unexpected pleasure, into the hours they spend with me.

Let me give them my best service and freest credit.

Let me keep my doors open to them at all hours.

Let my thoughts and words, which are my commodities, be always fresh and appealing.

May my friends never come to me for understanding and find it out of stock.

Let them never come to me for companionship and find it to be of poor quality.

May they never find my friendship to be more than they can afford, or even as much as they can afford.

Remind me never to deceive them with false advertisements of myself.

Thus, help me to be a "bargain" friend, O Lord, always.

And then if I find at last that I have given to them more than I've gotten in repayment, then I shouldn't at all mind going out of business that way.

James Alexander Thom

THE TROUBLE WITH SHARON

"The trouble with Sharon is that she never calls. Have you noticed that?"

I had noticed and had given it some thought. Sharon is one of my best friends and I talk to her or see her almost every week. But Sharon never calls me.

I don't think that means she isn't thinking of me. I'm pretty sure that I cross her mind fairly often. But Sharon just doesn't call people unless it's something important.

So what should I do? Keep track of my calls to her and if the score goes beyond 6-0, quit calling her?

What would that prove? Absolutely nothing and it might deprive me of a wise and loving friend.

Every friend has at least one flaw. I'm sure I have more than one. And Sharon hasn't dropped me because of them.

Friendship has got to be accepting, forgetful of what isn't perfect because of all that is. People who don't go along with that run the risk of losing something very precious.

It would be like throwing a diamond in the trash because you discover it has one tiny flaw. Worse than that. You can always pick up a new diamond at the jewelers, but you can never replace a friend.

Gayle Lawrence

SUCCESS

Success is being friendly *when another needs a friend . . .* It's in the cheery words you speak *and in the coins you lend . . .* Success is not alone in skill *and deeds of daring great . . .* It's in the roses that you plant *beside your garden gate . . .* Success is in the way you walk *the paths of life each day . . .* It's in the little things you do *and in the things you say . . .* Success is in the glad hello *you give your fellow man . . .* It's in the laughter of your home *and all the joys you plan . . .* Success is not in getting rich *or rising high to fame...* It's not alone in winning goals *which all men hope to claim . . .* It's in the person you are each day *through happiness or care . . .* It's in the happy words you speak *and in the smile you wear . . .* Success is being big of heart *and clean and broad of mind . . .* It's being faithful to your friends *and to the stranger, kind.*

Author Unknown

HUMAN NEED

Courage we need for this life of ours,
Courage, calmness, power;
Glee in the present which children own,
Hope for the coming hour.

Underneath, and all the time,
A warm pulse, beating
To Nature's beauty, loved one's rhythm,
The springtime urge repeating.

What will give us courage deep,
Joy in the things that are?
The true and lasting love of friends
For us, will go most far.

Madeline Benedict

TRIBUTE TO A DEAR FRIEND

A real and dear friend
Is a rare, precious blend
Of rapport, understanding, and trust;
Who knows of our tears
And our joys through the years,
With whom all our plans are discussed;

Dear friends are those
Who never disclose
The dreams we entrust to their keeping;
They watch through the night
Till the morning's first light—
While others care not, and are sleeping;

Dear friends never change,
We never feel strange
But always at home when they're near;
Friendships like these
Make fond memories
Which just grow increasingly dear;

Their worth can't be told
In silver or gold,
For love can't be measured on charts;
They've a most special place
Which time can't erase
In that one certain spot in our hearts!

Katherine Nelson Davis

The most agreeable of all companions is a simple, frank person, without any high pretensions to an oppressive greatness—one who loves life, and under-stands the use of it; obliging alike at all hours; above all, of a golden temper, and steadfast as an anchor. For such an one we gladly exchange the greatest genius, the most brilliant wit, the profoundest thinker.

Gotthold Ephraim Lessing

A FRIEND LISTENS

I have noted that the best and closest friends are those who seldom call on each other for help. In fact, such is almost the finest definition of a friend—a person who does not need us but who is able to enjoy us.

I have seldom suffered over the troubles of a friend. Are his mishaps short of tragedy, I am inclined to chuckle. And he is seldom serious in telling me of his misfortunes. He makes anecdotes out of them, postures comically in their midst and tries to entertain me with them. This is one of the chief values of my friendship, as it is of his. We enable each other to play the strong man superior to his fate. Given a friend to listen, my own disasters change color. I win victories while relating them. Not only have I a friend on my side who will believe my version of the battle—and permit me to seem a victor in my communiqúes—but I have actually a victory in me. I am able to show my friend my untouched side. My secret superiority to bad events becomes stronger when I can speak and have a friend believe in it.

Ben Hecht

SHARING THE GOOD AND BAD

We may describe friendly feeling towards any
one as wishing for him what you believe to be good
things, not for your own sake but for his, and being
inclined, so far as you can, to bring these things
about. A friend is one who feels thus and excites
these feelings in return: those who think they feel
thus towards each other think themselves friends.
This being assumed, it follows that your friend is the
sort of man who shares your pleasure in what is good
and your pain in what is unpleasant, for your sake
and for no other reason. This pleasure and pain of
his will be the token of his good wishes for you, since
we all feel glad at getting what we wish for, and
pained at getting what we do not. Those, then, are
friends to whom the same things are good and evil.

Aristotle

THE THIRD SELF OF FRIENDSHIP

"The meeting of two personalities is like the contact of two chemical substances; if there is any reaction, both are transformed."

Carl Jung

Friendship is a special kind of human experience.

One person might explain the special feeling by saying, "We understand each other because we're on the same wave length."

Another might say, "We are free to be ourselves with each other and don't have to worry about what people say."

A third: "Our friendship is like a protective cloud that surrounds us, and when we're together we feel safe, secure and trusting."

Or: "Whenever I'm with friends I'm open to new ideas and experiences and that is exciting."

The secret of that fresh, alive, open and excited feeling seems to be that friendship provides a chance to live a new life. "Friendship is a second existence," explained Baltasar Gracian.

People talk about friendship as if it had a life of its own: being born, growing, passing through crises, weakening and sometimes dying.

Perhaps this way of talking about friendship provides the most fundamental insight of all—that *friendship is a thing in itself,* that is real, unique and personal. It can be called a *third self,* a new reality distinct from the friends themselves.

Muriel James and Louis Savary

I WANT A FRIEND

I want a warm and faithful friend,
    To cheer the adverse hour;
Who ne'er to flatter will descend,
    Nor bend the knee to power;
A friend to chide me when I'm wrong,
    My inmost soul to see;
And that my friendship prove as strong
    To him as his to me.

John Quincy Adams

WHAT WE NEED

"A friend in need," my neighbor said to me—
    "A friend in deed is what I mean to be;
In time of trouble I will come to you
    And in the hour of need you'll find me true."

I thought a bit, and took him by the hand,
    "My friend," I said, "you do not understand
The inner meaning of that simple rhyme—
    A friend is what the heart needs all the time."

Author Unknown

Greater love hath no man than this, that a man lay down his life for his friends.

Ye are my friends, if ye do whatsoever I command you. Henceforth I call you not servants; for the servant knoweth not what his lord doeth: but I have called you friends.

. . . Ye have not chosen me, but I have chosen you.

John 15:13-16

We cannot tell the precise
moment when friendship is
formed.
As in filling a vessel drop by
drop, there is at last a drop
which makes the heart run over.

James Boswell

At eighteen, friendship is the buoyant acceptance of
those who play and work and laugh and dream together... As a man gets older, he wants friends to
stimulate him, to keep his mind active and young.

Bernard Baruch

TO RECEIVE

It is more blessed to give than to receive . . .
[But] the givers who cannot take in return miss one
of the finest graces in life, the grace of receiving . . . .
To receive gratefully from others is to enhance their
sense of their worth. It puts them on a give-and-take
level, the only level on which real fellowship can be
sustained . . . . It changes one of the ugliest things in
the world, patronage, into one of the richest things in
the world, friendship.

Halford E. Luccock

SHE IS MY FRIEND

She listens when I talk, but more than that, she always hears me. She hears the subtle shading in my voice that tells her what my words do not. She catches feelings, carefully concealed behind the words, and understands.

She is my friend, and so she doesn't damage my hurt pride by pointing out my frailties. She simply says a thoughtful word or two, and suddenly I'm able to accept, to speak aloud my worries and embarrassments. I talk to her, and, as I do, my confidence returns.

Her friendship once again has shored me up, and I can face my fears and laugh them down. How many times she's listened when I talk, and how I count on her to really hear me.

Raphael Marie Turnbull

THROUGH TIME AND DISTANCE . . .

I am in New York, looking down on Central Park from the twentieth floor of my hotel. I am waiting for my friend. She has arranged for a sitter and is taking the New Haven train into the city from the small Connecticut town we once shared so that we can have dinner together. I am a corporate vice-president now. I carry a briefcase. I travel around the country by plane. I wear expensive clothes. A knock on the door announces her arrival. I open it, and her radiant smile sweeps away everything—the briefcase, the clothes, the room—leaving only some essential me that even I do not understand. I am . . . the year we made the kids lobster costumes for the Fourth of July parade and won first prize. I am . . . shopping for Christmas toys at Bloomingdale's together. I am . . . a hundred diets shared and what-color-do-you-think-I-should-paint-the-bedroom and can-you-and-Bob-come-for-dinner-on-Saturday?

We fight to talk. We have always talked simultaneously, each determined to prevail, for as long as thirty seconds at a time. It is our only competition. I can talk to her endlessly about my children; she never grows weary of it, expects and receives the same indulgence from me. She is as pleased with the turns my life has taken as I am. There is no conflict for her between then and now. It is not that I have not changed, for the changes are many and deep, nor that she does not perceive them, but rather that she is pure love, pure acceptance. She is the friend/mother/sister that we all wish we had: the one who gives us support without diminishing our independence, and who gives us continuity without denying our changes. To be around her is to feel happy.

Nancy Eberle

May the trail of the wind leave its songs in your path,
May the sun light the sky where you stand;
May the pleasure of friendship be yours through the days,
With the clasp of a caring hand.

Virginia Covey Boswell

ACKNOWLEDGMENTS

The editor and the publisher have made every effort to trace the ownership of all copyrighted material and to secure permission from copyright holders of such material. In the event of any question arising as to the use of any material the publisher and editor, while expressing regret for inadvertent error, will be pleased to make the necessary corrections in future printings. Thanks are due to the following authors, publishers, publications and agents for permission to use the material indicated.

CONDE NAST PUBLICATIONS, INC., for an excerpt by Nancy Eberle from *Glamour Magazine*, volume 76, #7, July 1978. Copyright © 1978 by The Condé Nast Publications, Inc.

CORNELL UNIVERSITY PRESS, for an excerpt from *Are Men Equal?* by Henry Alonzo Myers. Copyright © 1945 by Henry Alonzo Myers.

DOUBLEDAY & COMPANY, INC., for "Life's Common Things" by Alice E. Allen from *Treasurehouse Of Inspirational Poetry And Prose.* Edited by A. L. Alexander. Copyright © 1966 by A. L. Alexander.

E. P. DUTTON, for an excerpt from *This Happy Place* by Bentz Plagemann. Copyright © 1970 by Bentz Plagemann.

FAMILY ALBUM, for "What Is A Friend" by Grace E. Easley from *The Family Album*, 10 Star Edition. Copyright © 1975 by The Family Album.

FARM JOURNAL, INC., for "Neighbors" by Philene Hammer, from *This Way of Life.* Edited by Maude Longwell. Copyright © 1971 by Farm Journal, Inc.

GOLDEN QUILL PRESS, for "Happiness" from *Lyrics For Living* by Alfred G. Walton. Copyright © 1963 by Alfred G. Walton.

HARCOURT BRACE JOVANOVICH, INC., for an excerpt from *Wind, Sand And Stars* by Antoine de Saint-Exupery. Copyright © 1939 by Antoine de Saint-Exupery, renewed 1967 by Lewis Galantiere.

Illustrated by Cooki Thier
Designed by Adair Wilson
Set in Korinna